THE NEW **DECADE SERIES**

SONGS OF T
1940s

🔊 100 Songs with Online Audio Backing Tracks

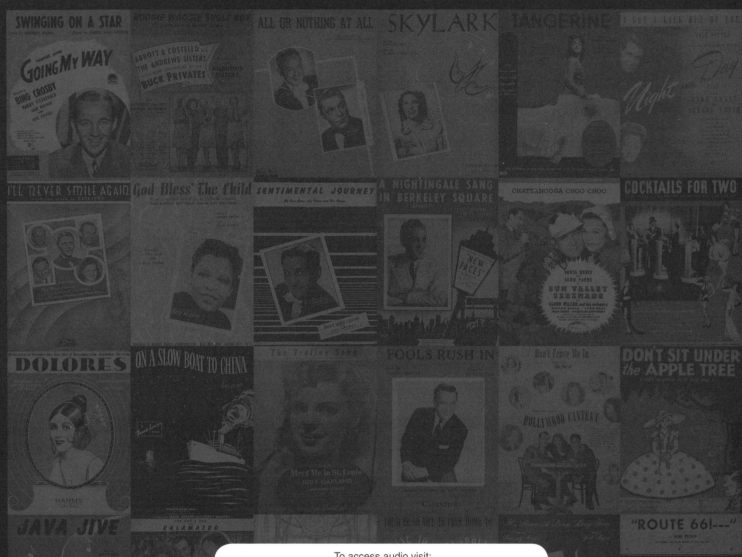

To access audio visit:
www.halleonard.com/mylibrary

Enter Code
2625-9492-9830-1048

ISBN 978-1-4950-0029-4

HAL•LEONARD®
CORPORATION

7777 W. BLUEMOUND RD. P.O. BOX 13819 MILWAUKEE, WI 53213

Visit Hal Leonard Online at
www.halleonard.com

AC-CENT-TCHU-ATE THE POSITIVE

Lyric by JOHNNY MERCER
Music by HAROLD ARLEN

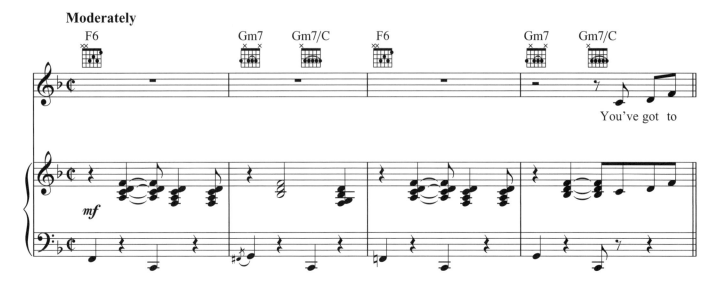

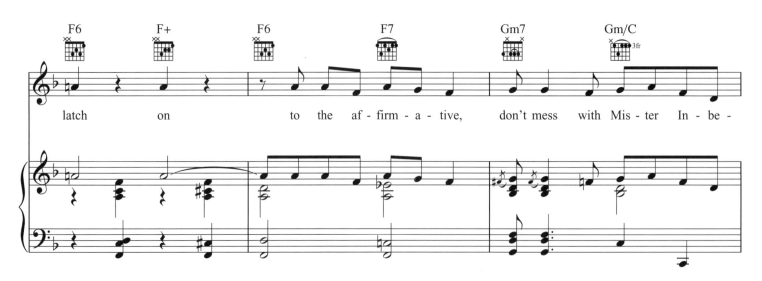

ACROSS THE ALLEY FROM THE ALAMO

Words and Music by
JOE GREENE

ALL OR NOTHING AT ALL

Words by JACK LAWRENCE
Music by ARTHUR ALTMAN

AMAPOLA
(Pretty Little Poppy)

By JOSEPH M. LACALLE
New English Words by ALBERT GAMSE

ALMOST LIKE BEING IN LOVE

Lyrics by ALAN JAY LERNER
Music by FREDERICK LOEWE

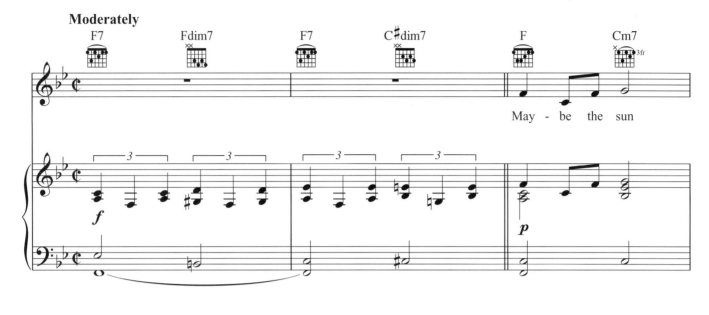

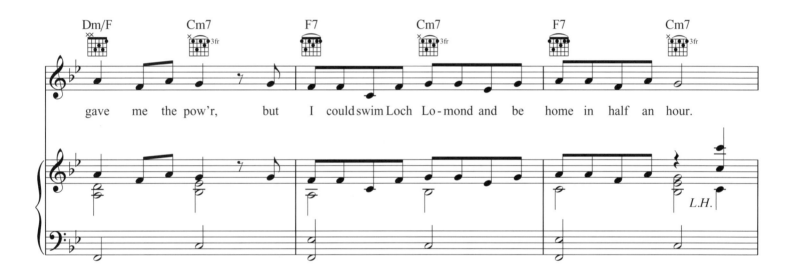

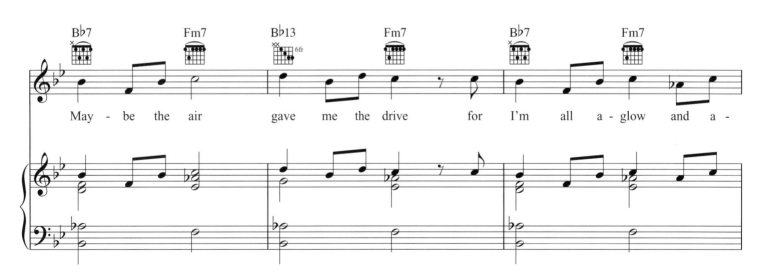

AQUELLOS OJOS VERDES
(Green Eyes)

Music by NILO MENENDEZ
Spanish Words by ADOLFO UTRERA
English Words by E. RIVERA and E. WOODS

Your green eyes with their
A - que - llos o - jos

AREN'T YOU GLAD YOU'RE YOU

Words by JOHNNY BURKE
Music by JIMMY VAN HEUSEN

BÉSAME MUCHO
(Kiss Me Much)

Music and Spanish Words by CONSUELO VELÁZQUEZ
English Words by SUNNY SKYLAR

Bé - sa - me, _____ bé - sa - me mu - cho, _____
Bé - sa - me, _____ bé - sa - me mu - cho, _____

each time I cling to your kiss I hear mu - sic di - vine. _____
co - mo si fue - ra es - ta no - che la úl - ti - ma vez; _____

Bé - sa - me mu - cho, _____
bé - sa - me mu - cho, _____

AT LAST

Lyric by MACK GORDON
Music by HARRY WARREN

BE CAREFUL, IT'S MY HEART

Words and Music by
IRVING BERLIN

Slowly, with expression

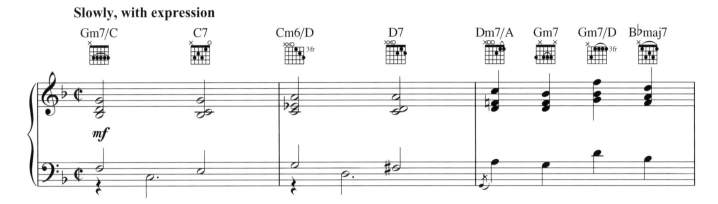

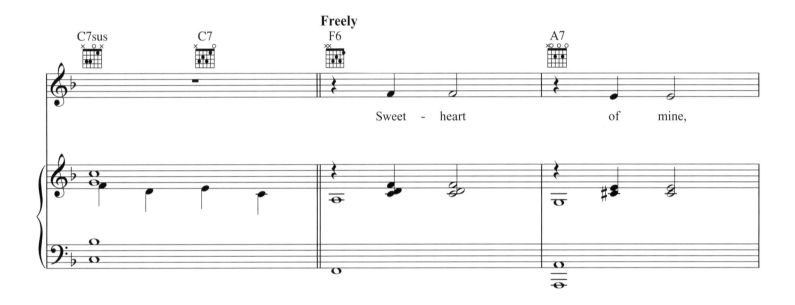

Sweet - heart of mine,

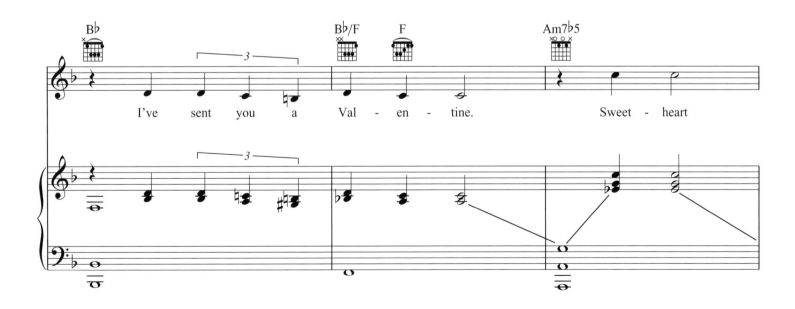

I've sent you a Val - en - tine. Sweet - heart

BEWITCHED

Words by LORENZ HART
Music by RICHARD RODGERS

BLUES IN THE NIGHT

Words by JOHNNY MERCER
Music by HAROLD ARLEN

BUT BEAUTIFUL

Words by JOHNNY BURKE
Music by JIMMY VAN HEUSEN

BOOGIE WOOGIE BUGLE BOY

Words and Music by DON RAYE
and HUGHIE PRINCE

Medium Boogie Woogie

He was a fa- mous trum- pet man from out Chi- ca- go way, ___ he had a "boo- gie" style that no one else could play. ___ He was the top man of his craft, ___

real - ly brought him down be - cause he could - n't jam.___ The cap - tain
wakes them up the same way in the ear - ly bright. ___ They clap their

seemed to un - der - stand, ___ be - cause the next day the "cap" ___ went out and
hands and stamp their feet ___ be - cause they know how he plays ___ when some - one

draft - ed a band.___ And now the com - p'ny jumps ⎱ when he plays re - veil - le, he's the
gives him a beat. ___ He real - ly breaks it up ⎰

boo - gie woo - gie bu - gle boy of Com - pa - ny B. ___ A toot! A toot! A

THE BREEZE AND I

Words by AL STILLMAN
Music by ERNESTO LECUONA

CANDY

Words and Music by MACK DAVID,
ALEX KRAMER and JOAN WHITNEY

Can-dy, I call my sug-ar Can-dy be-cause I'm sweet on Can-dy and Can-dy's sweet on me. {He}{She} un-der-

CHATTANOOGA CHOO CHOO

Lyric by MACK GORDON
Music by HARRY WARREN

COCKTAILS FOR TWO

Words and Music by ARTHUR JOHNSTON
and SAM COSLOW

COME RAIN OR COME SHINE

Words by JOHNNY MERCER
Music by HAROLD ARLEN

COW-COW BOOGIE

Words and Music by DON RAYE,
GENE DePAUL and BENNY CARTER

DADDY

Words and Music by
BOB TROUP

B♭ Cm7 F9 B♭ Gm7
Dad - dy! I want a brand - new car, cham - pagne,
Cm7 F9 1 B♭ Cm7 F9
cav - i - ar. Dad - dy! You ought - a get the best for
B♭ Cm7 F9 2 B♭
me. Hey! Dad - dy!
B♭dim Cm7 F9 B♭
Dad - dy! You ought - a get the best for me.
3fr

DAY BY DAY

Theme from the Paramount Television Series DAY BY DAY

Words and Music by SAMMY CAHN,
AXEL STORDAHL and PAUL WESTON

DO NOTHIN' TILL YOU HEAR FROM ME

Words and Music by DUKE ELLINGTON
and BOB RUSSELL

DOLORES

Words by FRANK LOESSER
Music by LOUIS ALTER

DON'T FENCE ME IN

Words and Music by
COLE PORTER

DON'T GET AROUND MUCH ANYMORE

Words and Music by DUKE ELLINGTON
and BOB RUSSELL

A DREAM IS A WISH YOUR HEART MAKES

from Walt Disney's CINDERELLA

Words and Music by MACK DAVID,
AL HOFFMAN and JERRY LIVINGSTON

DON'T SIT UNDER THE APPLE TREE
(With Anyone Else but Me)

Words and Music by LEW BROWN,
SAM H. STEPT and CHARLIE TOBIAS

DREAM

Words and Music by
JOHNNY MERCER

Slowly, with expression

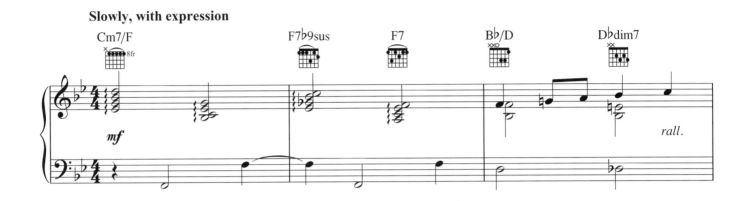

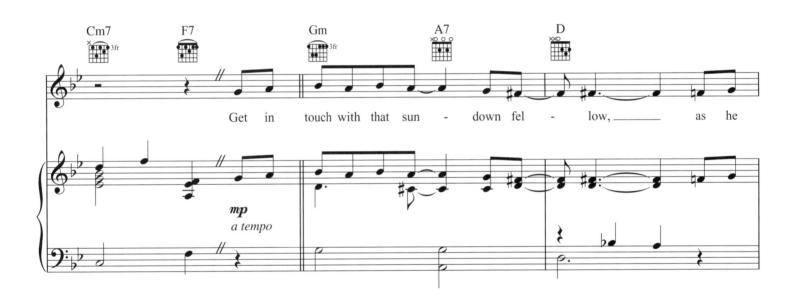

Get in touch with that sun - down fel - low, _____ as he

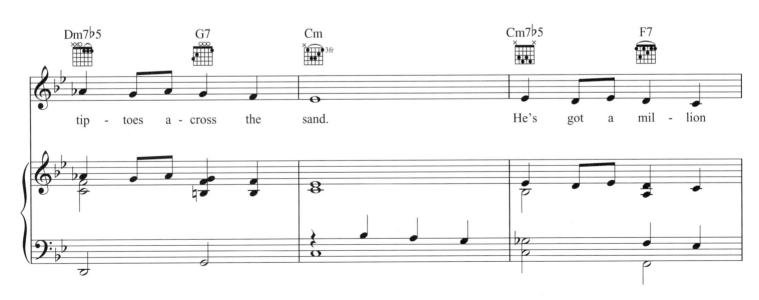

tip - toes a - cross the sand. He's got a mil - lion

FOOLS RUSH IN
(Where Angels Fear to Tread)

Lyrics by JOHNNY MERCER
Music by RUBE BLOOM

Moderately slow, with expression

(I Love You)
FOR SENTIMENTAL REASONS

Words by DEEK WATSON
Music by WILLIAM BEST

GOD BLESS' THE CHILD

Words and Music by ARTHUR HERZOG JR.
and BILLIE HOLIDAY

Them that's got shall get, them that's not shall lose, so the Bi-ble said, and it still is news. Ma-ma may have, Pa-pa may have, but God bless' the child that's got his own, that's got his own.

When you're gone and spend-in' ends, _ they don't come no more. Rich re-

la-tions give crust of bread and such. You can help your-self, but don't take too much!

Ma-ma may have, Pa-pa may have, but God bless' the child that's got his own, that's

1 got his own. Them that's got his own.

2 got his own. _

HOW HIGH THE MOON

Words by NANCY HAMILTON
Music by MORGAN LEWIS

125

HEARTACHES

Words by JOHN KLENNER
Music by AL HOFFMAN

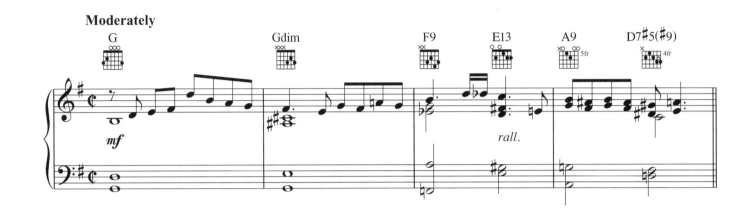

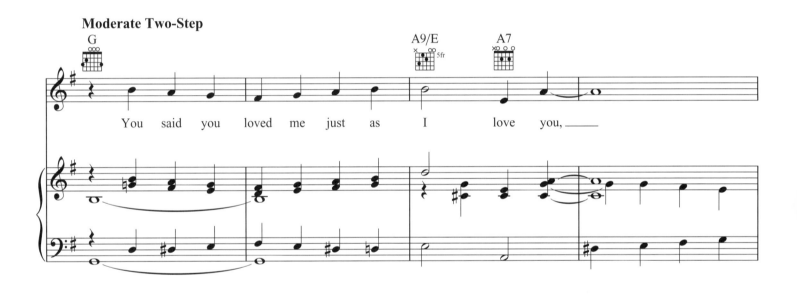

You said you loved me just as I love you, ____

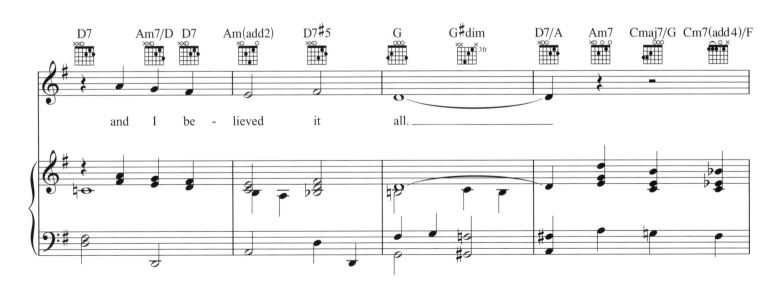

and I be-lieved it all. ____

HOW ARE THINGS IN GLOCCA MORRA

Words by E.Y. "YIP" HARBURG
Music by BURTON LANE

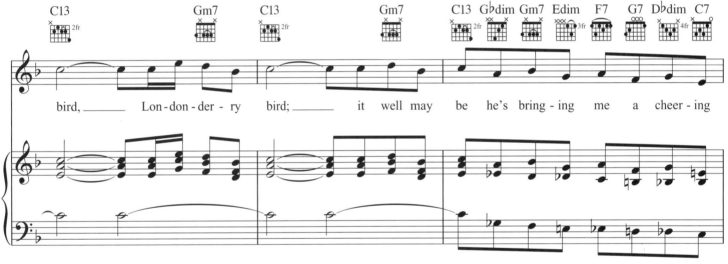

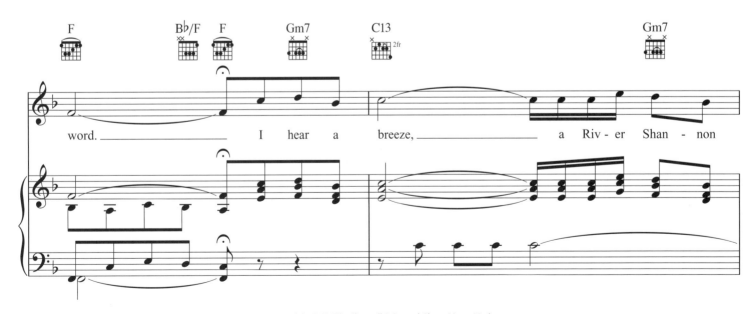

I CAN DREAM, CAN'T I?

Lyric by IRVING KAHAL
Music by SAMMY FAIN

I DON'T WANT TO SET THE WORLD ON FIRE

Words by EDDIE SEILER and SOL MARCUS
Music by BENNIE BENJAMIN and EDDIE DURHAM

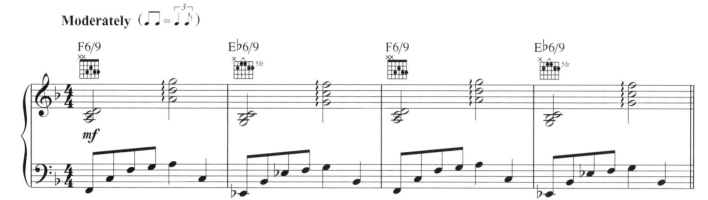

I don't want to set the world on fire.
In my heart I have but one de - sire,

I just want to start a flame in your heart.
and that one is you;

I COULD WRITE A BOOK

Words by LORENZ HART
Music by RICHARD RODGERS

I GET A KICK OUT OF YOU

Words and Music by
COLE PORTER

I GOT IT BAD AND THAT AIN'T GOOD

Words by PAUL FRANCIS WEBSTER
Music by DUKE ELLINGTON

I WISH I DIDN'T LOVE YOU SO

Words and Music by
FRANK LOESSER

I REMEMBER YOU

Words by JOHNNY MERCER
Music by VICTOR SCHERTZINGER

I'LL BE AROUND

Words and Music by
ALEC WILDER

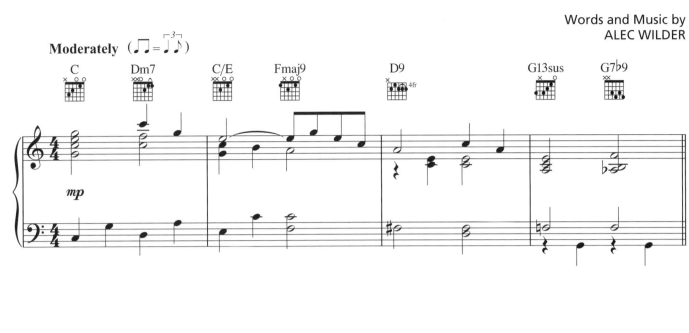

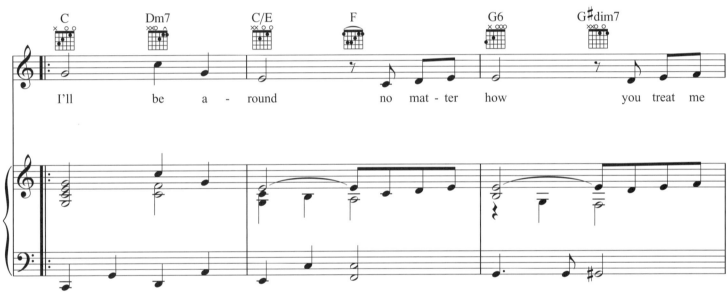

I'll be a - round no mat - ter how you treat me

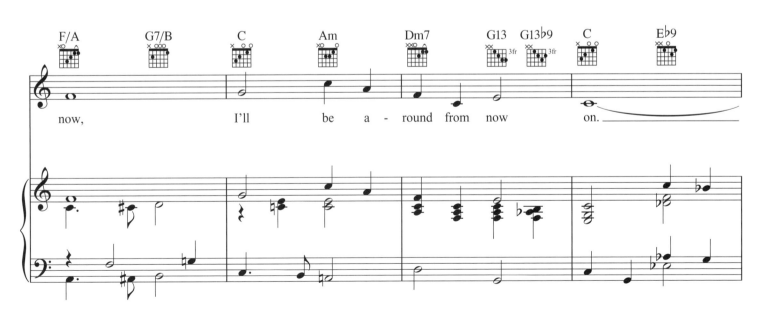

now, I'll be a - round from now on.

I'LL NEVER SMILE AGAIN

Words and Music by
RUTH LOWE

I'M BEGINNING TO SEE THE LIGHT

Words and Music by DON GEORGE, JOHNNY HODGES,
DUKE ELLINGTON and HARRY JAMES

IN THE BLUE OF EVENING

Words by TOM ADAIR
Music by D'ARTEGA

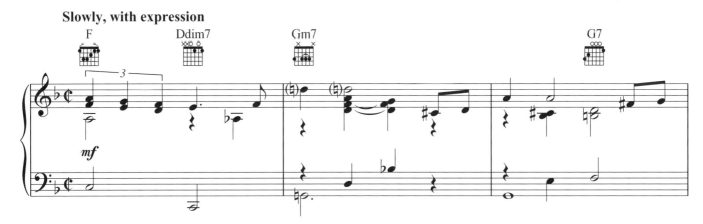

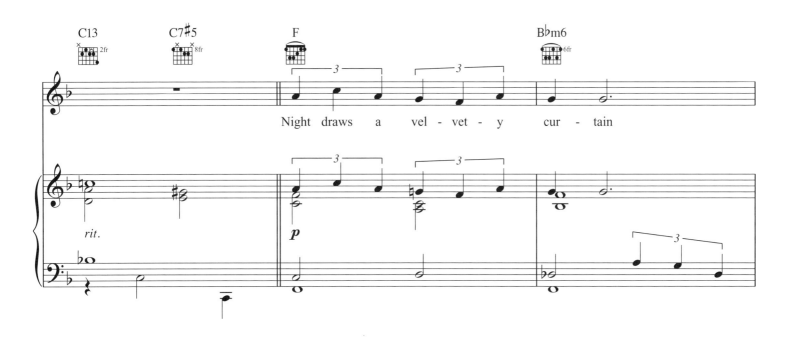

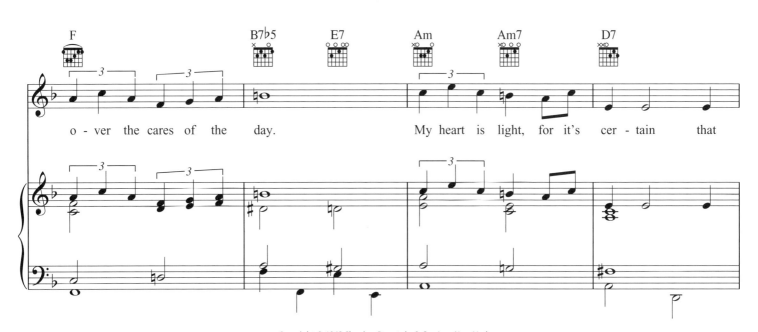

I'll be meet-ing you in se-cret ren-dez-vous: In the blue of

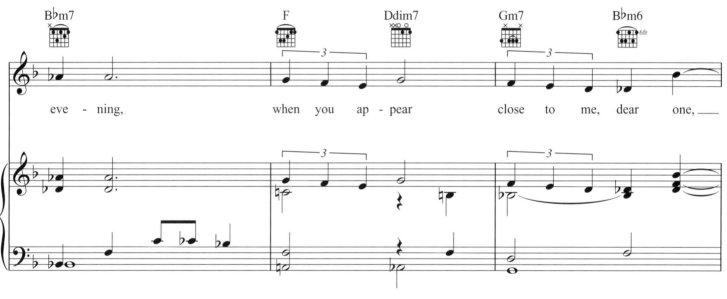

eve - ning, when you ap-pear close to me, dear one, ___

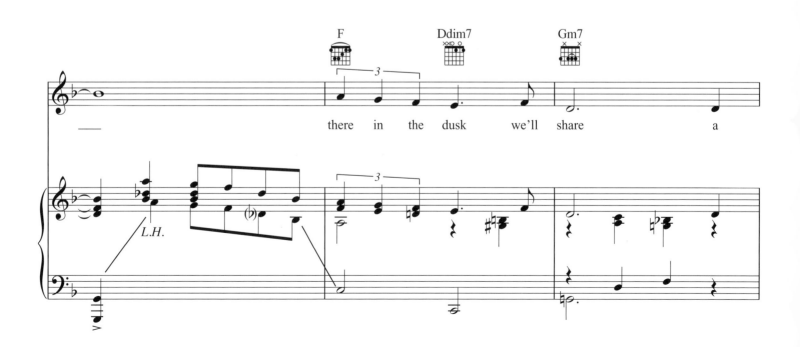

___ there in the dusk we'll share a

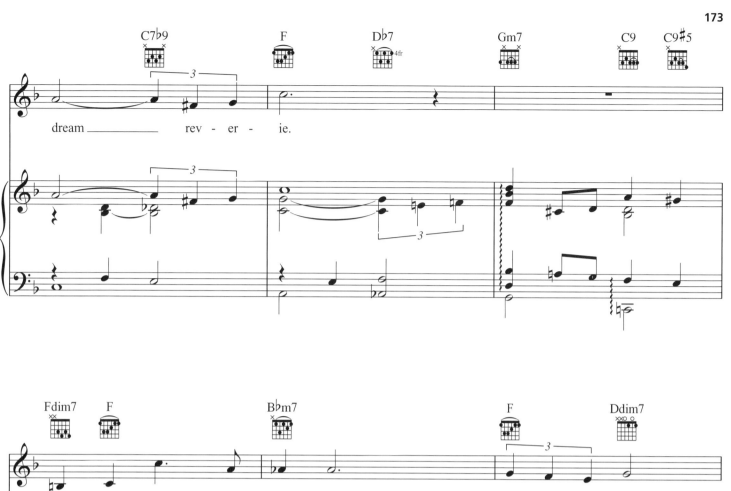

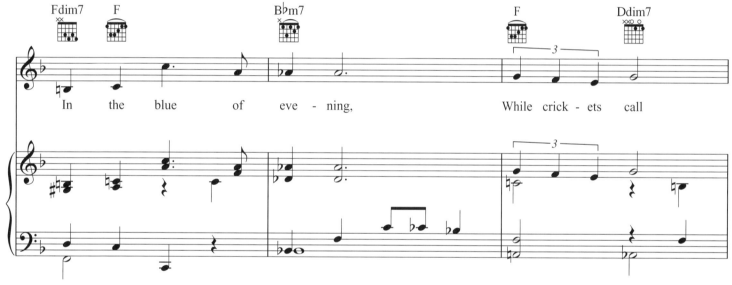

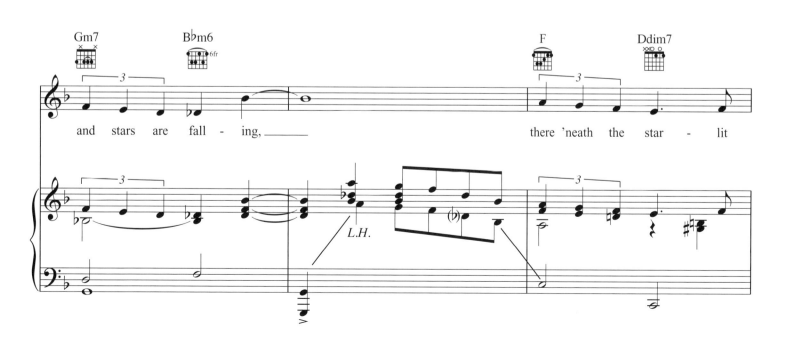

I'M OLD FASHIONED

Lyrics by JOHNNY MERCER
Music by JEROME KERN

I'VE GOT A GAL IN KALAMAZOO

from the film ORCHESTRA WIVES

Words by MACK GORDON
Music by HARRY WARREN

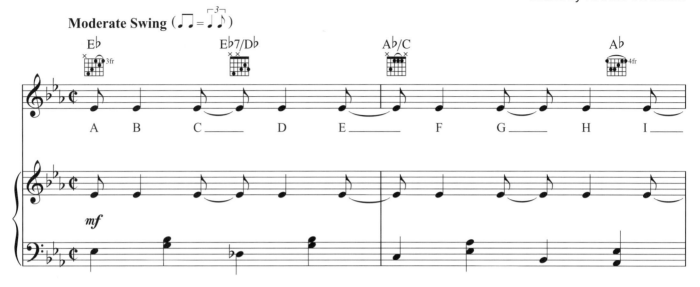

A B C D E F G H I

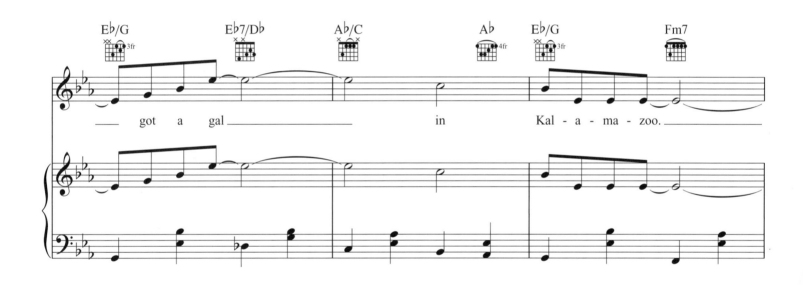

got a gal in Kal - a - ma - zoo.

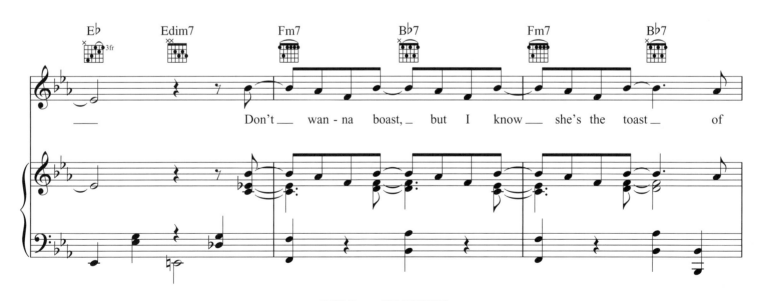

Don't wan - na boast, but I know she's the toast of

I'VE HEARD THAT SONG BEFORE

Lyric by SAMMY CAHN
Music by JULE STYNE

IT COULD HAPPEN TO YOU

Words by JOHNNY BURKE
Music by JAMES VAN HEUSEN

IT MIGHT AS WELL BE SPRING

from STATE FAIR

Lyrics by OSCAR HAMMERSTEIN II
Music by RICHARD RODGERS

Moderately

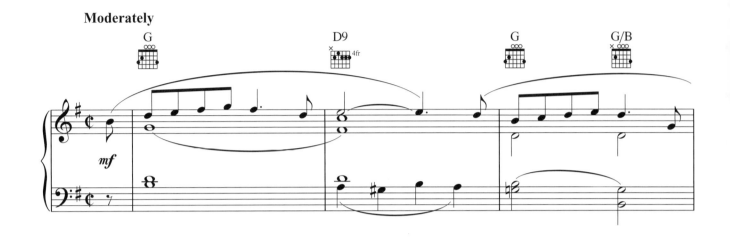

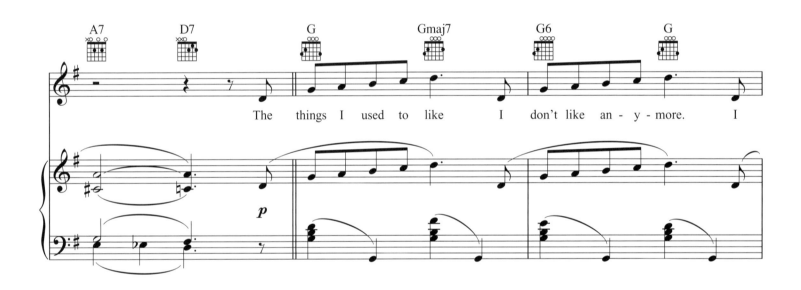

The things I used to like I don't like an-y-more. I want a lot of oth-er things I've

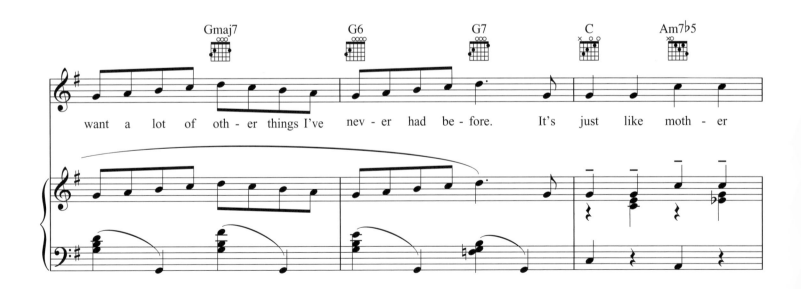

nev-er had be-fore. It's just like moth-er

IT'S BEEN A LONG, LONG TIME

Lyric by SAMMY CAHN
Music by JULE STYNE

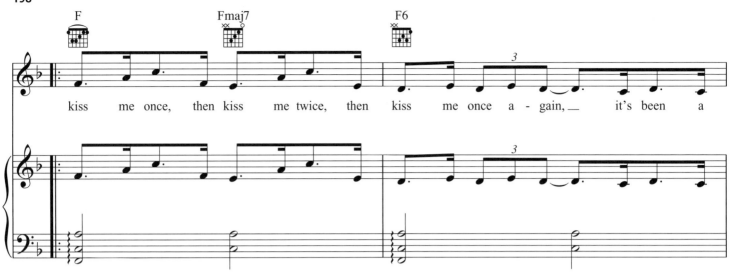

kiss me once, then kiss me twice, then kiss me once a - gain, __ it's been a

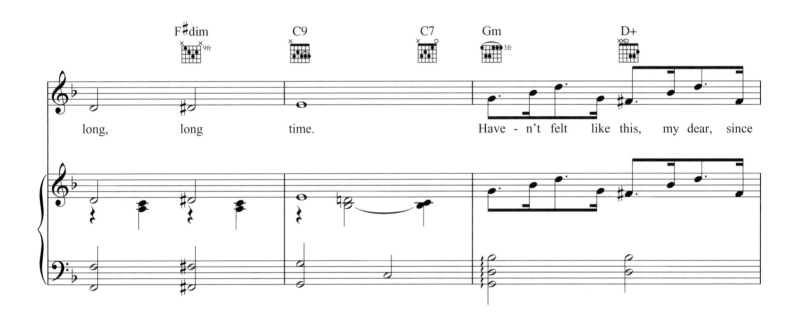

long, long time. Have - n't felt like this, my dear, since

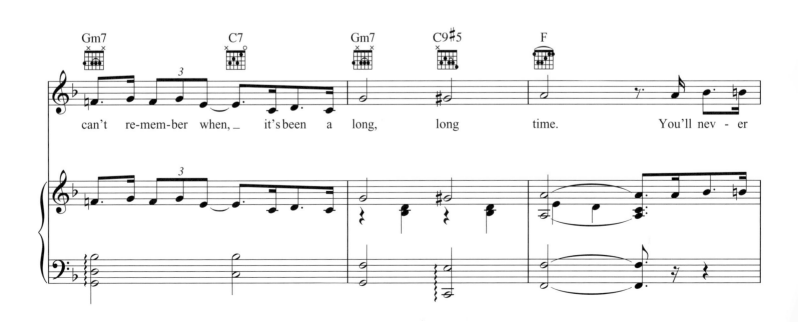

can't re-mem-ber when, __ it's been a long, long time. You'll nev - er

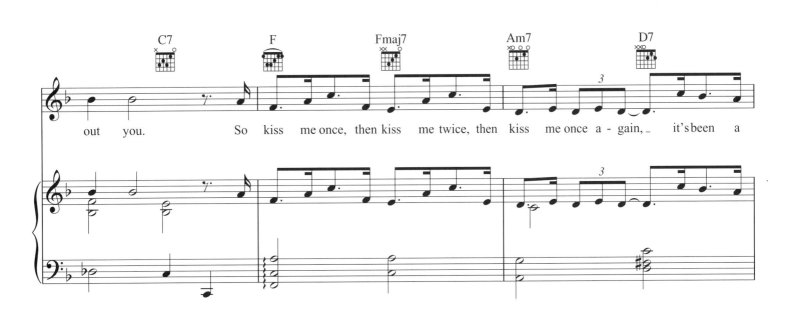

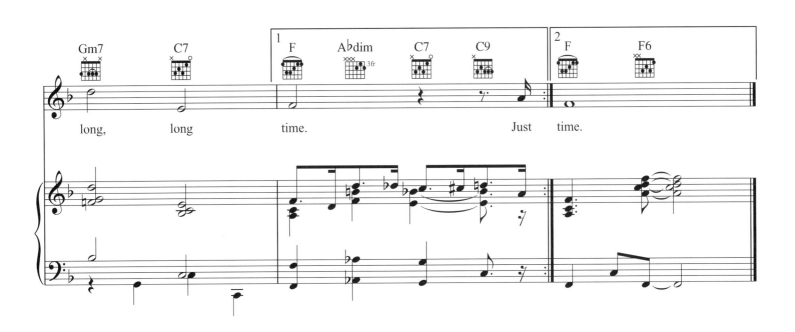

IT NEVER ENTERED MY MIND

Words by LORENZ HART
Music by RICHARD RODGERS

JAVA JIVE

Words and Music by MILTON DRAKE
and BEN OAKLAND

JUST SQUEEZE ME
(But Don't Tease Me)

Words by LEE GAINES
Music by DUKE ELLINGTON

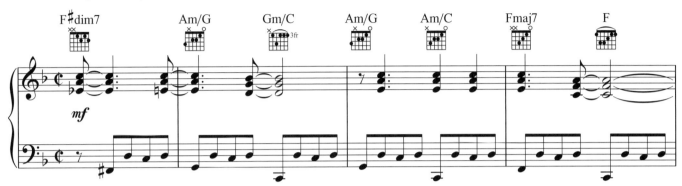

Want you to know I go for your squeez- in'.

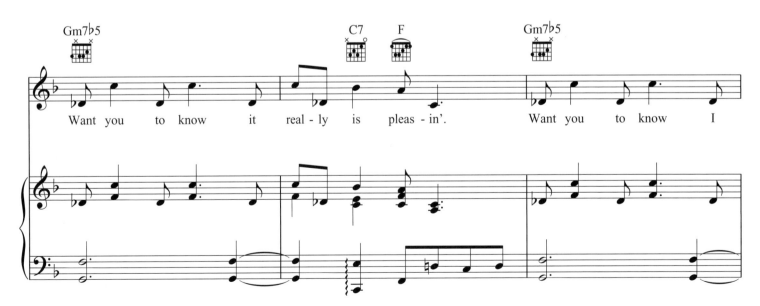

Want you to know it real- ly is pleas- in'. Want you to know I

LA VIE EN ROSE
(Take Me to Your Heart Again)

Original French Lyrics by EDITH PIAF
Music by LUIS GUGLIELMI
English Lyrics by MACK DAVID

Hold me close and hold me
Quand il me prend dans ses

fast, the mag-ic spell you cast, this is la vie en
bras, Il me par-le tout bas, Je vois la vie en

rose._____ When you kiss me heav-en
ro - se, Il me dit des mots d'a-

THE LAST TIME I SAW PARIS

Lyrics by OSCAR HAMMERSTEIN II
Music by JEROME KERN

The

last time I saw Par - is, her heart was warm and gay. I

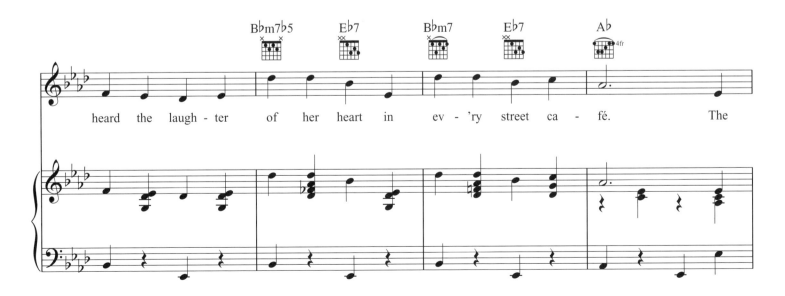

heard the laugh - ter of her heart in ev - 'ry street ca - fé. The

LAURA

Lyric by JOHNNY MERCER
Music by DAVID RAKSIN

MAIRZY DOATS

Words and Music by MILTON DRAKE,
AL HOFFMAN and JERRY LIVINGSTON

Lightly

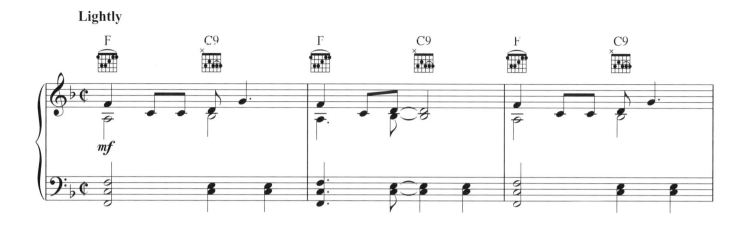

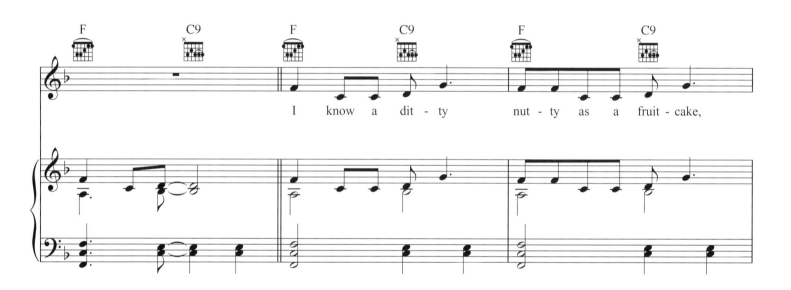

I know a dit-ty nut-ty as a fruit-cake,

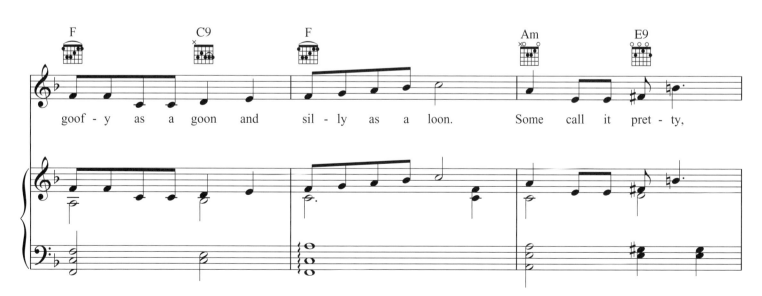

goof-y as a goon and sil-ly as a loon. Some call it pret-ty,

LET THERE BE LOVE

Lyric by IAN GRANT
Music by LIONEL RAND

LIKE SOMEONE IN LOVE

Words by JOHNNY BURKE
Music by JIMMY VAN HEUSEN

LOVER MAN
(Oh, Where Can You Be?)

By JIMMY DAVIS,
ROGER RAMIREZ and JIMMY SHERMAN

NATURE BOY

Words and Music by
EDEN AHBEZ

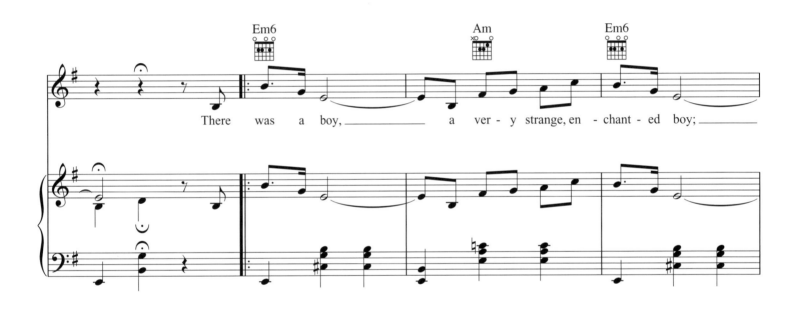

There was a boy, _____ a ver-y strange, en-chant-ed boy; _____

_____ they say he wan-dered ver-y far, ver-y far

A NIGHTINGALE SANG IN BERKELEY SQUARE

Lyric by ERIC MASCHWITZ
Music by MANNING SHERWIN

*Pronounced "Bar-kley"

NEAR YOU

Words by KERMIT GOELL
Music by FRANCIS CRAIG

THE OLD LAMPLIGHTER

Words by CHARLES TOBIAS
Music by NAT SIMON

He made the night ___ a lit-tle bright-er wher-

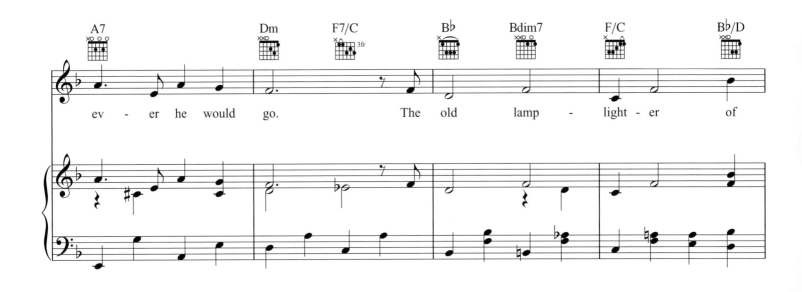

ev-er he would go. The old lamp-light-er of

long, long a-go. ___ His snow-y hair ___ was so much
night ___ a lit-tle

ON A SLOW BOAT TO CHINA

By FRANK LOESSER

ON THE ATCHISON, TOPEKA AND THE SANTA FE

Words by JOHNNY MERCER
Music by HARRY WARREN

ONCE IN LOVE WITH AMY

By FRANK LOESSER

Once in love with A - my, — al - ways in love with A - my, — ev - er and ev - er fas - ci - nat - ed by 'er, sets your heart a - fire — to stay.

258

ONE FOR MY BABY
(And One More for the Road)

Lyric by JOHNNY MERCER
Music by HAROLD ARLEN

PEOPLE WILL SAY WE'RE IN LOVE

Lyrics by OSCAR HAMMERSTEIN II
Music by RICHARD RODGERS

PERFIDIA

Words and Music by
ALBERTO DOMÍNGUEZ

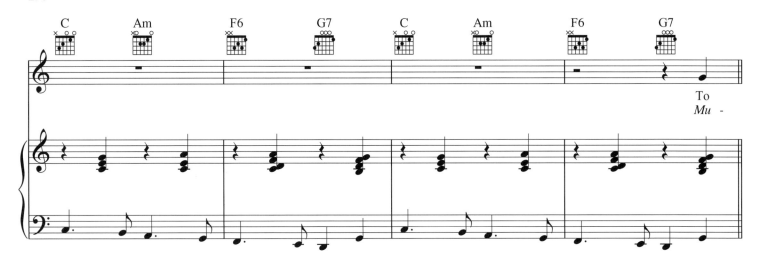

To
Mu -

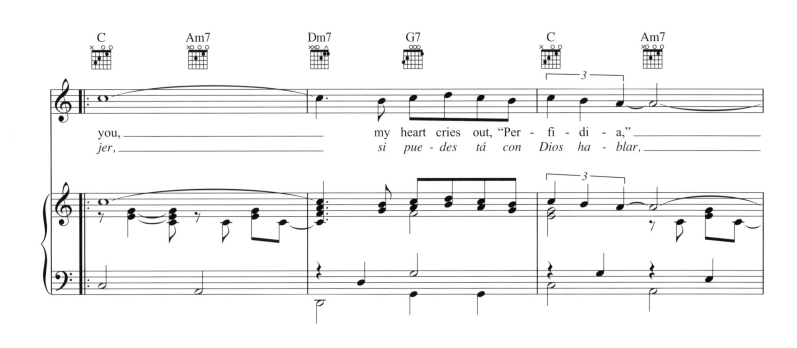

you, _____ my heart cries out, "Per - fi - di - a," _____
jer, _____ *si pue - des tá con Dios ha - blar,* _____

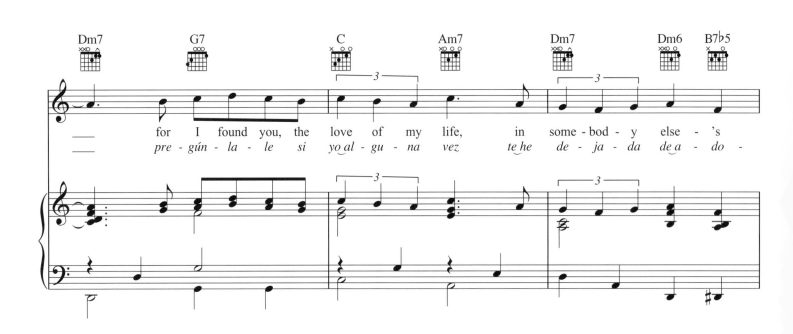

___ for I found you, the love of my life, in some - bod - y else - 's
___ *pre - gún - la - le si yo al - gu - na vez te he de - ja - da de a - do -*

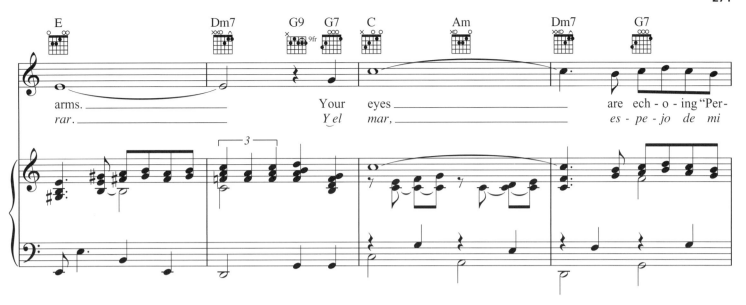

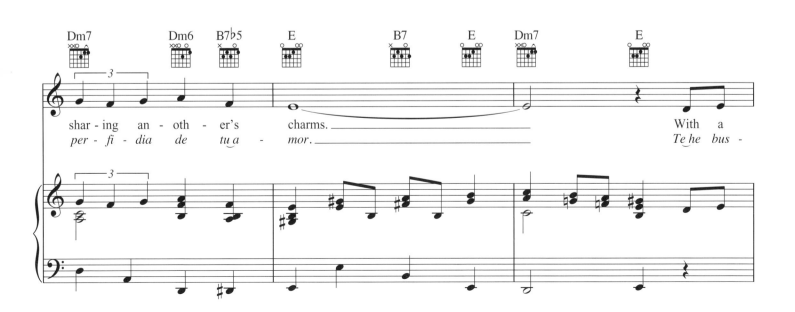

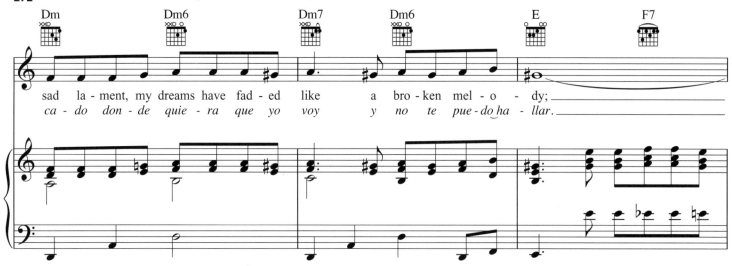

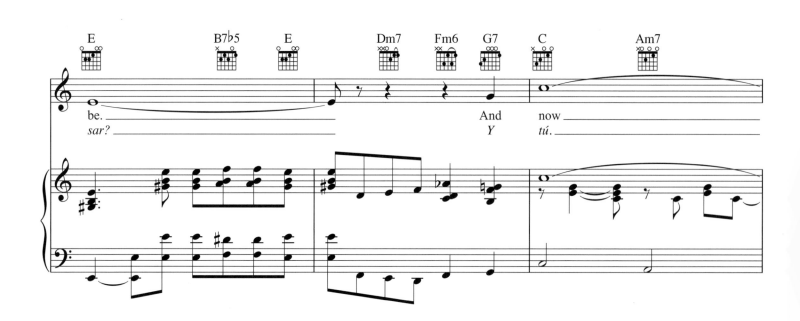

PISTOL PACKIN' MAMA

Words and Music by
AL DEXTER

Moderate Western Two-Step

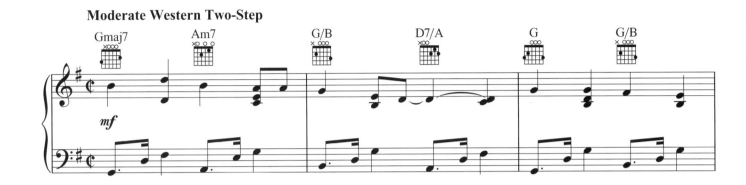

Drink - in' beer in a cab - a - ret, ___ and
She kicked out my ___ wind - shield, ___ she
Drink - in' beer in a cab - a - ret, ___ and

was I hav - in' fun! Un - til one night she
hit me o - ver the head, she cussed and cried she and
danc - ing with a blonde, un - til one night she

POINCIANA
(Song of the Tree)

Words by BUDDY BERNIER
Music by NAT SIMON

Moderately, with expression

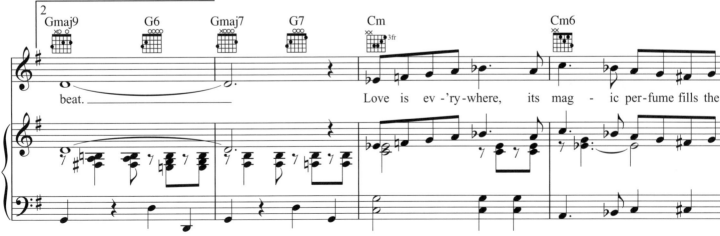

an - a, _____ your branch-es speak to me of love. _____
an - a, _____ some-how I feel the jun-gle heat. _____ With-

Pale moon _____ is cast-ing shad-ows from a - bove. _____ Poin - ci -
in me _____ there grows a rhyth-mic sav-age

beat. _____ Love is ev-'ry-where, its mag - ic per-fume fills the

ROUTE 66

By BOBBY TROUP

SENTIMENTAL JOURNEY

Words and Music by BUD GREEN,
LES BROWN and BEN HOMER

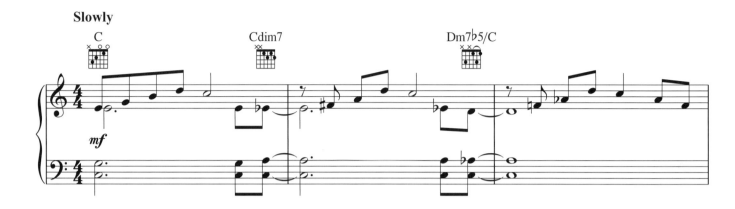

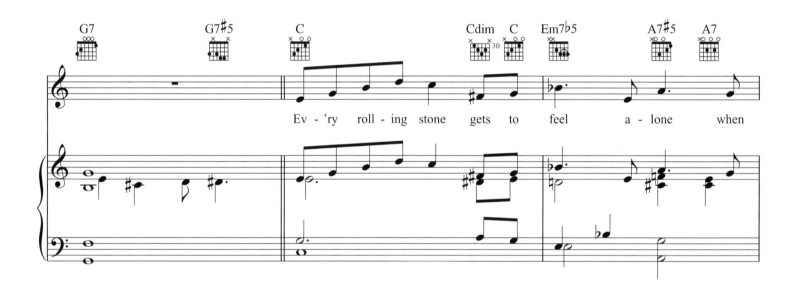

Ev - 'ry roll - ing stone gets to feel a - lone when

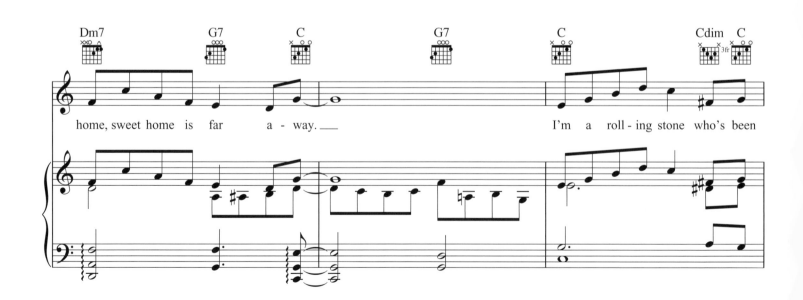

home, sweet home is far a - way. ___ I'm a roll - ing stone who's been

SKYLARK

Words by JOHNNY MERCER
Music by HOAGY CARMICHAEL

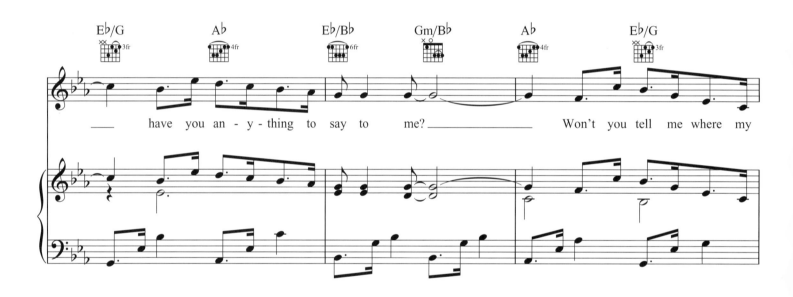

SO IN LOVE
from KISS ME, KATE

Words and Music by
COLE PORTER

Moderato

Strange, dear, _____ but true, dear, _____ when I'm close _____ to you, dear, _____

SOME ENCHANTED EVENING

Lyrics by OSCAR HAMMERSTEIN II
Music by RICHARD RODGERS

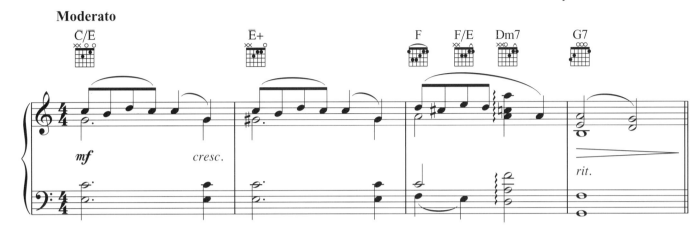

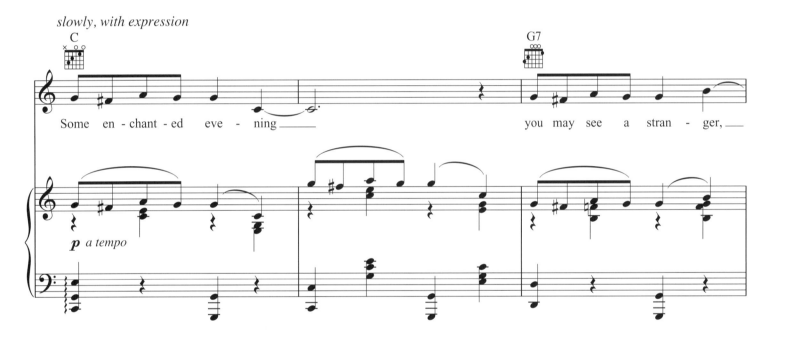

Some en-chant-ed eve-ning _____ you may see a stran-ger,

_____ you may see a stran-ger _____ a-cross a

SOMEBODY ELSE IS TAKING MY PLACE

Words and Music by DICK HOWARD,
BOB ELLSWORTH and RUSS MORGAN

SPEAK LOW

Words by OGDEN NASH
Music by KURT WEILL

THE SURREY WITH THE FRINGE ON TOP

Lyrics by OSCAR HAMMERSTEIN II
Music by RICHARD RODGERS

Brightly

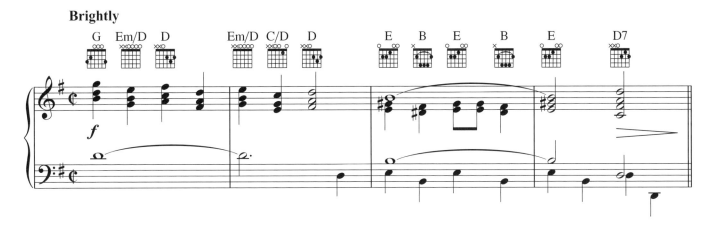

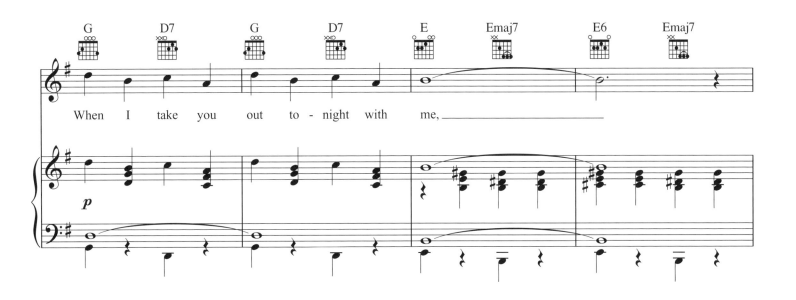

When I take you out to-night with me, _____

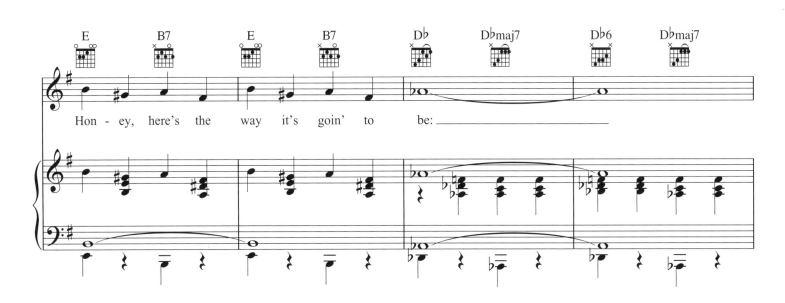

Hon-ey, here's the way it's goin' to be: _____

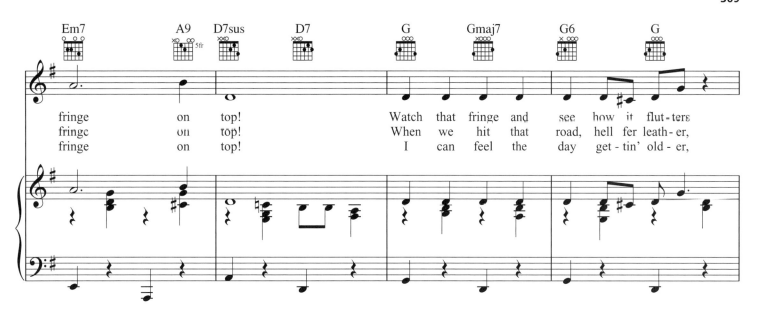

fringe on top! Watch that fringe and see how it flut-ters
fringe on top! When we hit that road, hell fer leath-er,
fringe on top! I can feel the day get-tin' old-er,

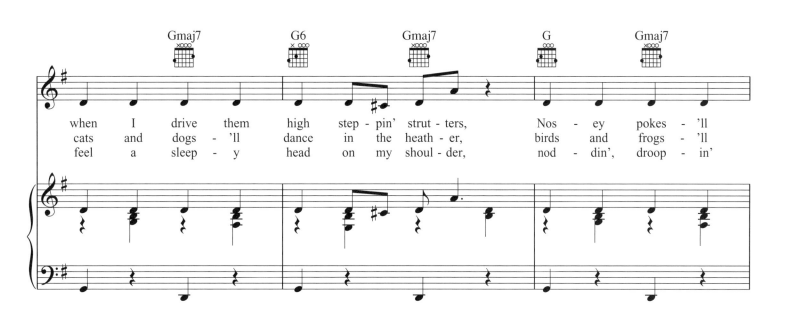

when I drive them high step-pin' strut-ters, Nos-ey pokes-'ll
cats and dogs-'ll dance in the heath-er, birds and frogs-'ll
feel a sleep-y head on my shoul-der, nod-din', droop-in'

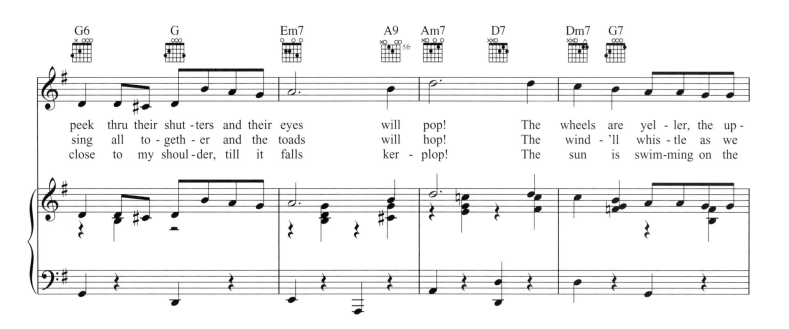

peek thru their shut-ters and their eyes will pop! The wheels are yel-ler, the up-
sing all to-geth-er and the toads will hop! The wind-'ll whis-tle as we
close to my shoul-der, till it falls ker-plop! The sun is swim-ming on the

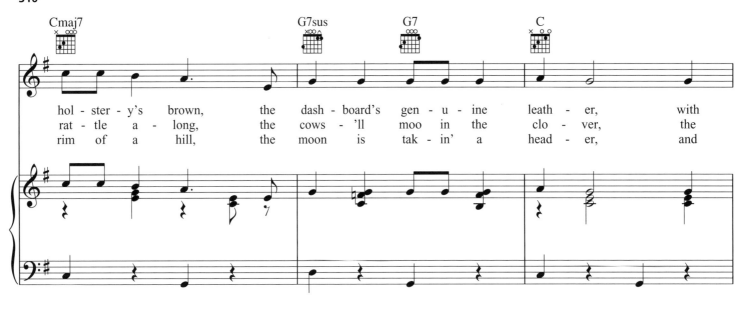

hol - ster - y's brown, the dash - board's gen - u - ine leath - er, with
rat - tle a - long, the cows - 'll moo in the clo - ver, the
rim of a hill, the moon is tak - in' a head - er, and

is - in - glass cur - tains y' can roll right down, in case there's a change in the
riv - er will rip - ple out a whis - pered song, and whis - per it o - ver and
jist as I'm think - in' all the earth is still, a lark - 'll wake up in the

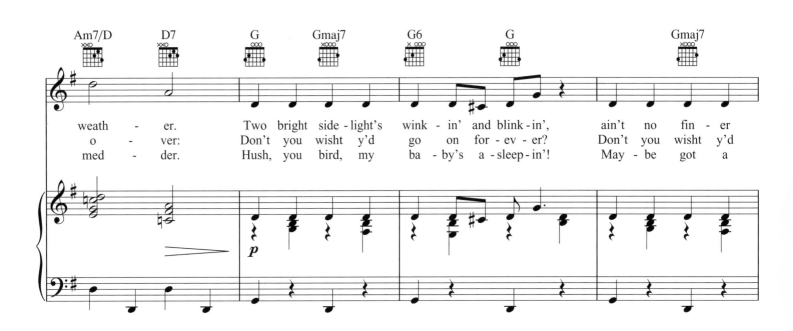

weath - er. Two bright side - light's wink - in' and blink - in', ain't no fin - er
o - ver: Don't you wisht y'd go on for - ev - er? Don't you wisht y'd
med - der. Hush, you bird, my ba - by's a - sleep - in'! May - be got a

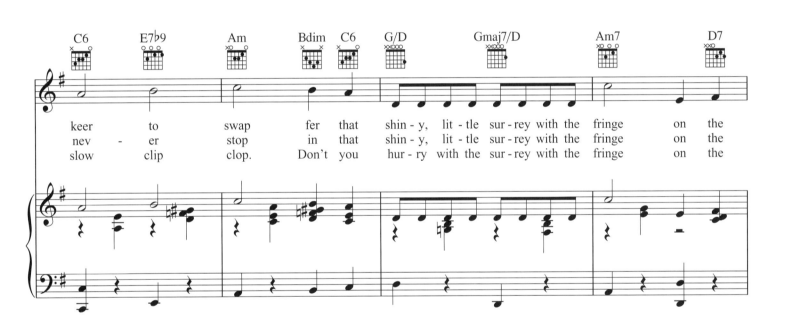

STEPPIN' OUT WITH MY BABY

Words and Music by
IRVING BERLIN

STRAIGHTEN UP AND FLY RIGHT

Words and Music by NAT KING COLE
and IRVING MILLS

A STRING OF PEARLS

Words by EDDIE DE LANGE
Music by JERRY GRAY

SWINGING ON A STAR

Words by JOHNNY BURKE
Music by JIMMY VAN HEUSEN

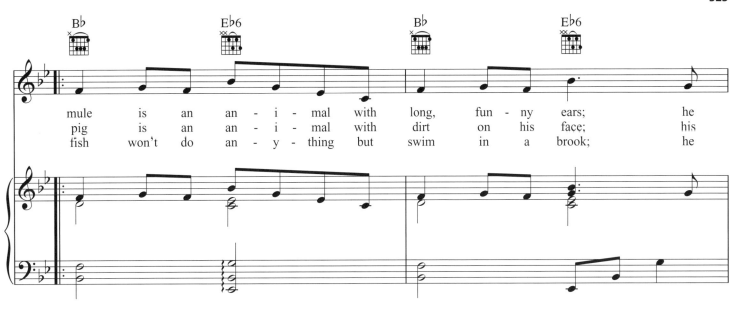

mule is an an - i - mal with long, fun - ny ears; he
pig is an an - i - mal with dirt on his face; his
fish won't do an - y - thing but swim in a brook; he

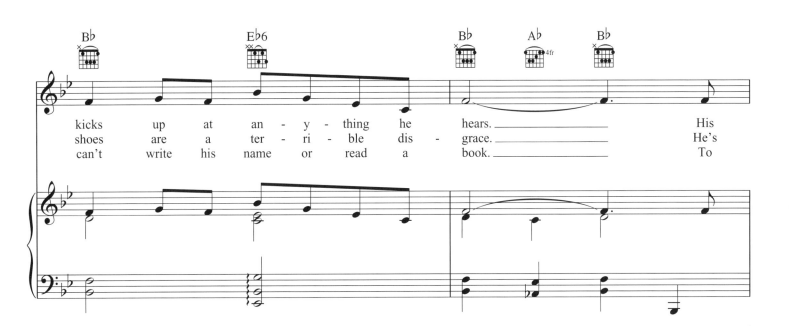

kicks up at an - y - thing he hears. _____ His
shoes are a ter - ri - ble dis - grace. _____ He's
can't write his name or read a book. _____ To

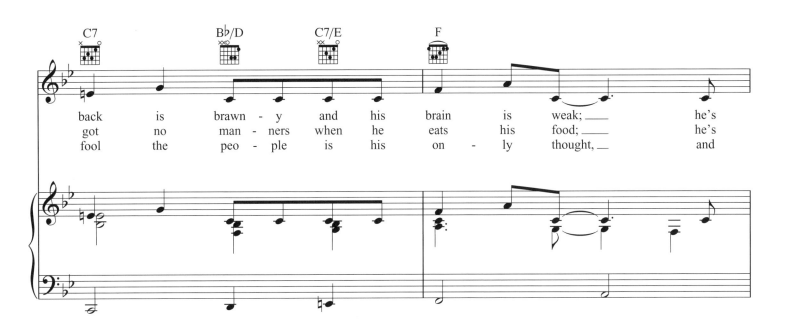

back is brawn - y and his brain is weak; ____ he's
got no man - ners when he eats his food; ____ he's
fool the peo - ple is his on - ly thought, _ and

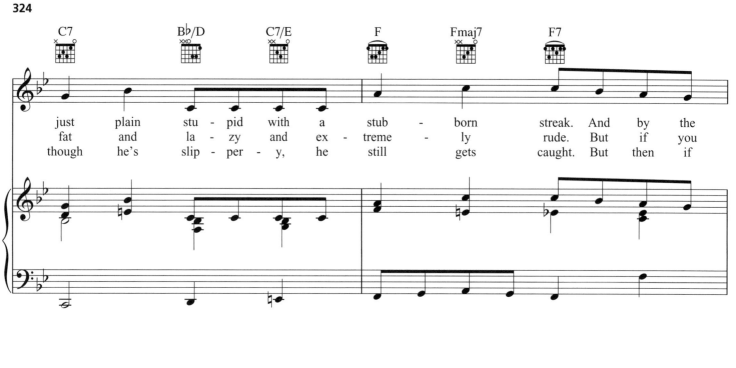

just plain stu - pid with a stub - born streak. And by the
fat and la - zy and ex - treme - ly rude. But if you
though he's slip - per - y, he still gets caught. But then if

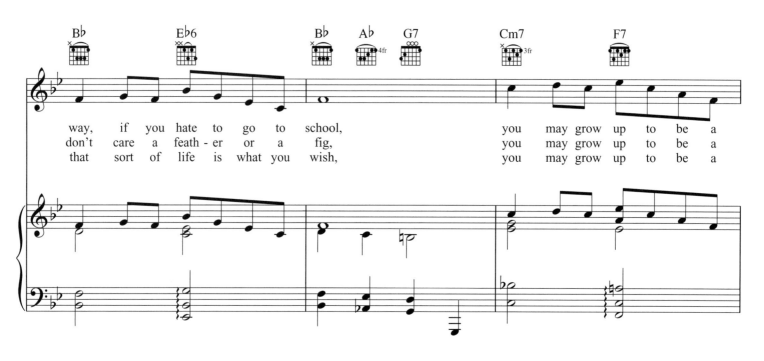

way, if you hate to go to school, you may grow up to be a
don't care a feath - er or a fig, you may grow up to be a
that sort of life is what you wish, you may grow up to be a

mule. _____ Or would you like to swing on a star, car - ry
pig. _____ Or would you like to swing on a star, car - ry
fish. _____ And all the mon - keys aren't in the zoo; ev - 'ry

TAKING A CHANCE ON LOVE

Words by JOHN LA TOUCHE and TED FETTER
Music by VERNON DUKE

Lyrics:

I thought love's game was o-ver La-dy Luck had gone a-way. I laid my cards on the ta-ble un-a-ble to play then I heard good for-tune say, _____ "They're

TANGERINE

Words by JOHNNY MERCER
Music by VICTOR SCHERTZINGER

South A-mer-i-can sto-ries ____ tell of a girl who's quite a dream, ____ the beau-ty of her race. Though you doubt all the sto-ries ____ and think the tales are just a bit ex-

THAT OLD BLACK MAGIC

Words by JOHNNY MERCER
Music by HAROLD ARLEN

THE THINGS WE DID LAST SUMMER

Words by SAMMY CAHN
Music by JULE STYNE

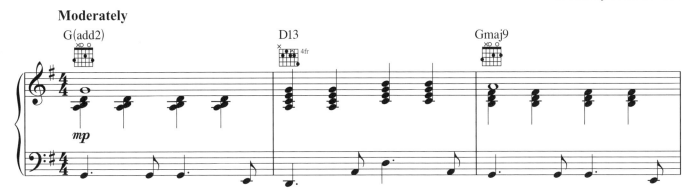

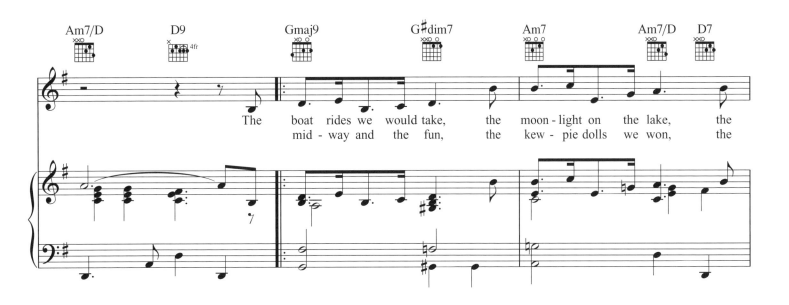

The boat rides we would take, the moon-light on the lake, the
mid-way and the fun, the kew-pie dolls we won, the

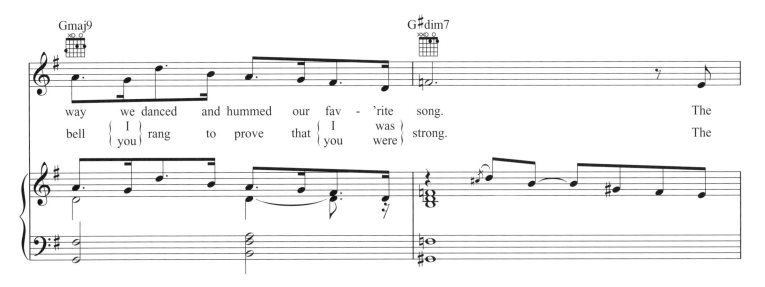

way we danced and hummed our fav-'rite song.
bell {I/you} rang to prove that {I was/you were} strong.

The
The

THEY SAY IT'S WONDERFUL

Words and Music by
IRVING BERLIN

TIME AFTER TIME

Words by SAMMY CAHN
Music by JULE STYNE

What good are words I say to you? ____ ____ They can't con-vey to you ____ what's in my heart. ____ If you could hear ____

THE TROLLEY SONG

Words and Music by HUGH MARTIN
and RALPH BLANE

351

WHEN YOU WISH UPON A STAR

Words by NED WASHINGTON
Music by LEIGH HARLINE

TUXEDO JUNCTION

Words by BUDDY FEYNE
Music by ERSKINE HAWKINS,
WILLIAM JOHNSON and JULIAN DASH

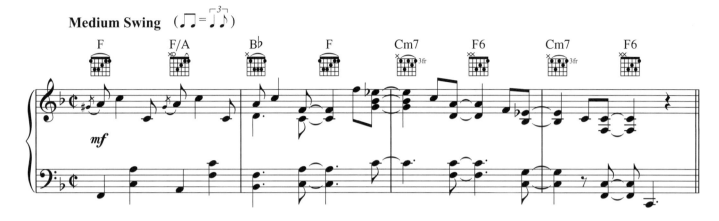

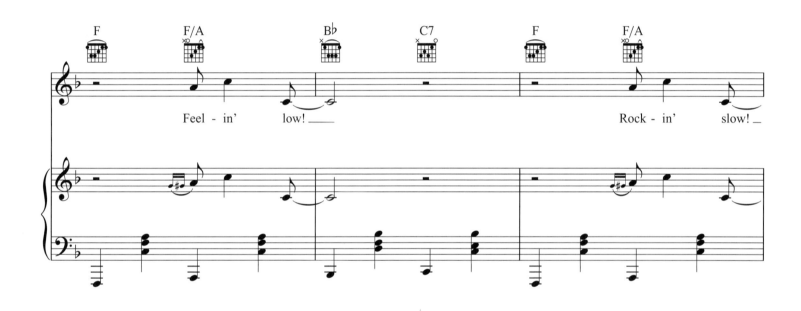

Feel - in' low! _____ Rock - in' slow! _

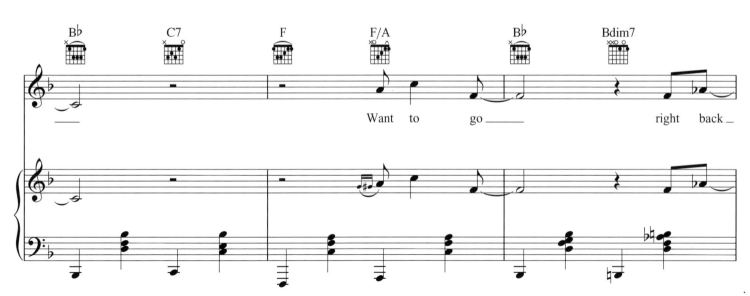

Want to go _____ right back _

WHY DON'T YOU DO RIGHT

(Get Me Some Money, Too!)

By JOE McCOY

YES INDEED

Words and Music by
SY OLIVER

YOU MADE ME LOVE YOU
(I Didn't Want to Do It)

Words by JOE McCARTHY
Music by JAMES V. MONACO

I've been wor- ried all day long, ___
I had pic- tured in my mind, ___

ZIP-A-DEE-DOO-DAH

Words by RAY GILBERT
Music by ALLIE WRUBEL

This is just the kind of day that you dream a-bout, ____ when you o-pen up your mouth a song pops out.

Zip - a-dee-doo - dah, zip - a-dee-ay! ____

YOU'D BE SO NICE TO COME HOME TO

Words and Music by
COLE PORTER